24 Introits

AND INTRODUCTORY SENTENCES

by ERIC H. THIMAN

NOVELLO PUBLISHING LIMITED

Order No: NOV 030105

CONTENTS

Where no organ part is included, these introits should be sung unaccompanied.

Eric H. Thiman

24 INTROITS

AND INTRODUCTORY SENTENCES

For SATB Choir & Organ

NOVELLO

To the Choir of the City Temple, London

Twenty-four Introits
and
Introductory Sentences
SET TO MUSIC BY
ERIC H. THIMAN

1

18958

2

Allegro
From the ris - ing of the sun un - til the go - ing down of the
Allegro
Ped.

allarg.
The Lord's name be prais'd.
same,
The Lord's name be prais'd, be prais'd.

The Lord's name be prais'd, the Lord's name be prais'd.
The Lord's name be prais'd, the Lord's name be prais'd.

allarg.

3

Andante
God
Bless - ed is the na - tion whose God

is
p
is the Lord, and the peo - ple whom he hath
p

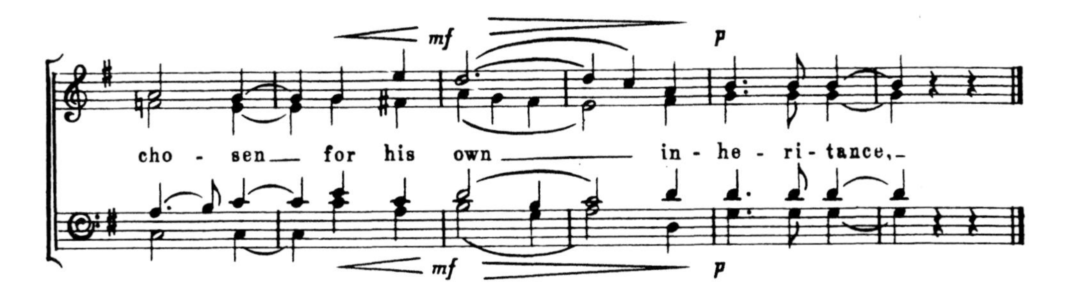
mf
p
cho - sen for his own in - he - ri - tance,
mf
p

4

Tranquillo
p
mp
I wait for the Lord, my soul doth wait for
p
mp

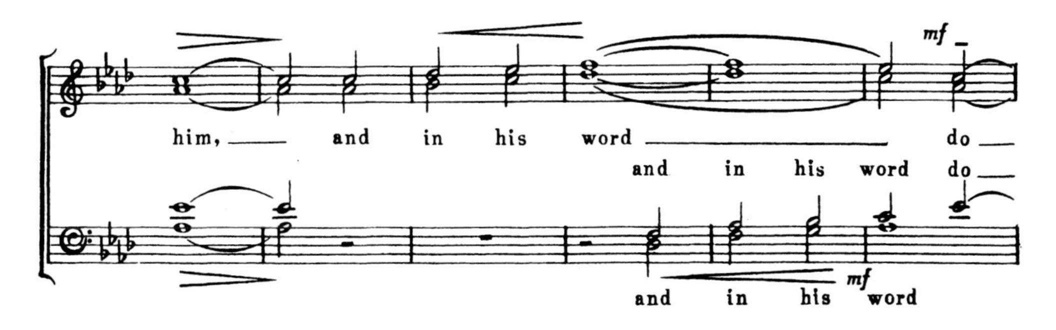
mf
him, and in his word do
and in his word do
mf
and in his word

p
rall.
pp
I hope, do I hope.
do I hope, do I hope.
p
pp

5

Allegro vivace

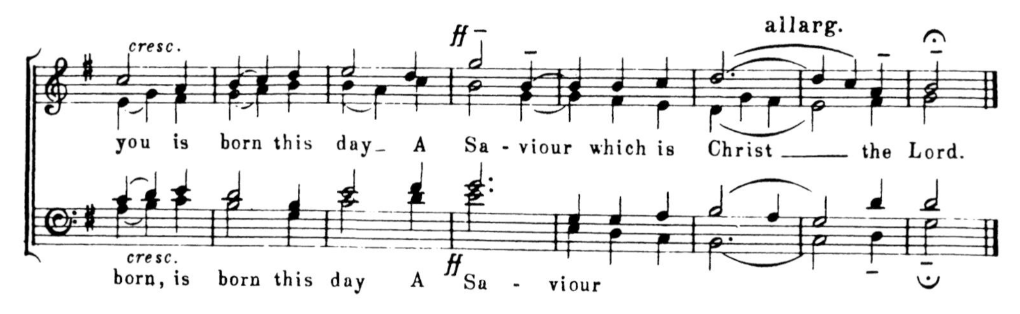

6

Andante

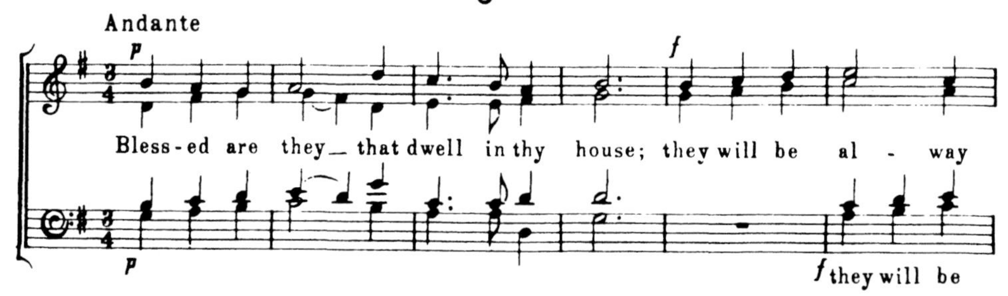

7

Maestoso
I was glad when they said un-to me,
Maestoso
Ped.

let us go in-to the house of the Lord:
Our feet shall
Our feet shall stand, shall

Our feet shall stand with-in thy gates,
allarg.
stand with - in thy gates, O Je - ru - sa - lem.
stand with - in thy gates,
allarg.

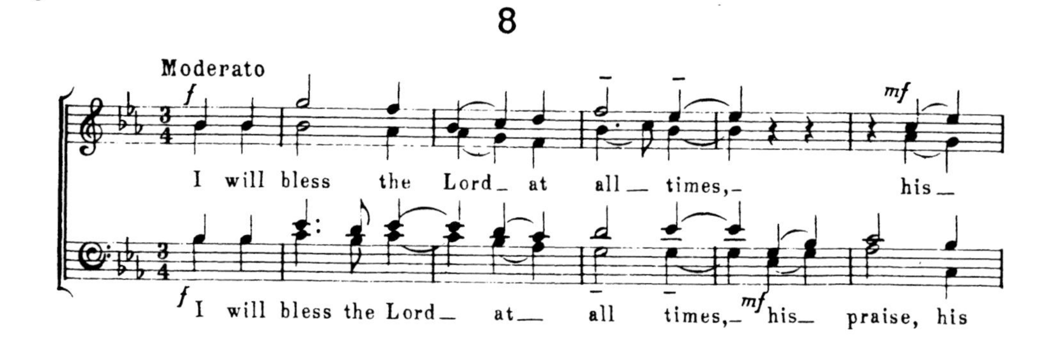
8
Moderato
I will bless the Lord _ at all _ times, _ his _
I will bless the Lord _ at _ all times, _ his _ praise, his

praise _ shall be _ con - tin - ual - ly _ in my mouth. _

9

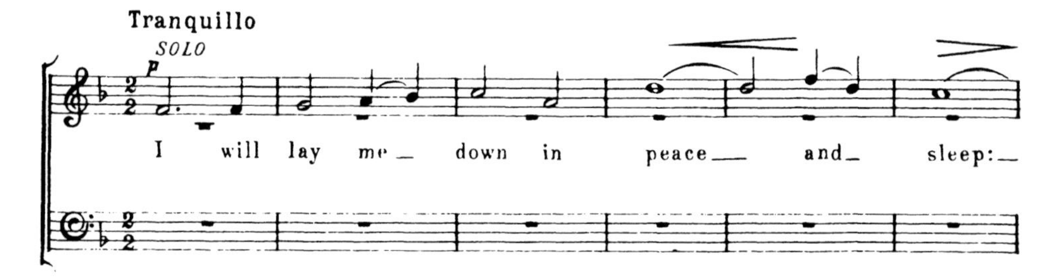
Tranquillo
SOLO
I will lay me _ down in peace _ and _ sleep: _

FULL
I _ will lay me _ down in peace _ and _ sleep: _

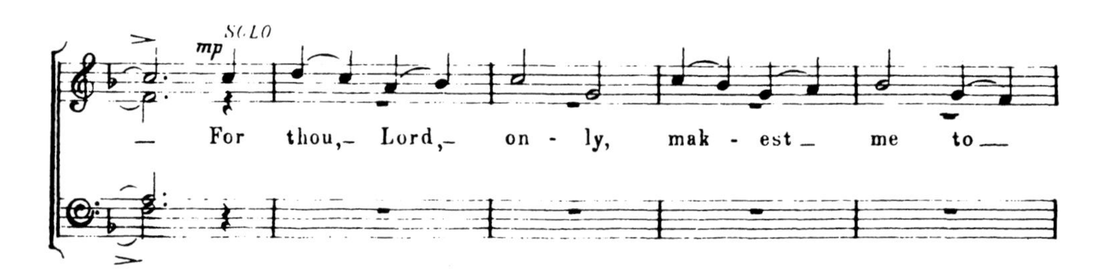
SOLO
_ For thou, _ Lord, _ on - ly, mak - est _ me to _

FULL
mf
dwell in safe - ty. For thou,— Lord, on - ly,—
mf

to— dwell in safe - ty.
pp
mak - est— me— to— dwell in safe - ty.
pp
to dwell in safe - ty.

10

Moderato
p
the hills,
I will lift up mine eyes un - to the hills, un - to the
p I will lift up mine eyes un - to the hills, un - to the

mf
hills, from whence com - eth my help.— My help cometh ev - en from the
hills,
mf My help cometh ev - en from the

p
rall.
Lord, who hath made— heav'n and earth, who hath made heav'n and earth.
Lord,
p

11

Con spirito
Lift up your heads,
Con spirito
mf (Sw. reeds)
Man.
f (Gt.)
Ped.
O ye gates, Even lift them up ye ev-er-last-ing
Man.

and the King of glo-ry
doors: and the King, and the King of glo-ry
and the King,
mf and the King of glo-ry, f and the King of glo-ry
mf
f
Ped.

shall come in.
shall come in.
shall come in.
mf Who is this King of glo - ry?
(Sw.)
Man.
mf
Who is this King of glo - ry?
f The Lord of hosts,
(Ch.)
f (Sw. reeds)
f
the Lord of hosts, he is the King of glo - ry.
ff
allarg.
ff
allarg.
ff (Gt)
Ped.

12

Andante, solenne
Lord, thou hast been our dwell - ing place in
Andante, solenne
(soft reed)
p (Gt.)
Ped. poco marcato

all __ gen - er - a - tions. Be - fore the moun - tains were brought

cresc.
forth or ev - er thou hadst form'd the earth and the world,
cresc.
cresc.

p
f cresc.
even from everlasting to everlasting,
mf

ff
f
poco rall.
rall.
thou art God, thou art God.

13

Allegro
f
O give thanks unto the Lord,
Ped.

mf
for his mercy endureth for ever.
for he is good;
mf
Man.
Ped.
mf
for his mercy en-
f O give thanks unto the God of Gods,
3
f
mf
Man.
cresc.
dureth for ever, for ever, for ev-
mf for his mercy endureth for ever,
cresc.
f
cresc.
Ped.
ff
allarg.
er, for his mercy endureth for ever.
ff
allarg.
ff
3

14

Moderato
are the Lord's:
The heav'n, ev-en the heav'ns, are the Lord's, are the Lord's: but the

rall.
earth hath he giv'n to the chil - dren of men.

15

Andante
Seek ye My face,
Seek ye My face,
SOLO
When thou saidst, Seek ye, My face,
Seek ye My face,

SOLO
My heart said un-to thee, FULL
thy face, Lord, will I

seek, thy face, Lord, will I seek.

16

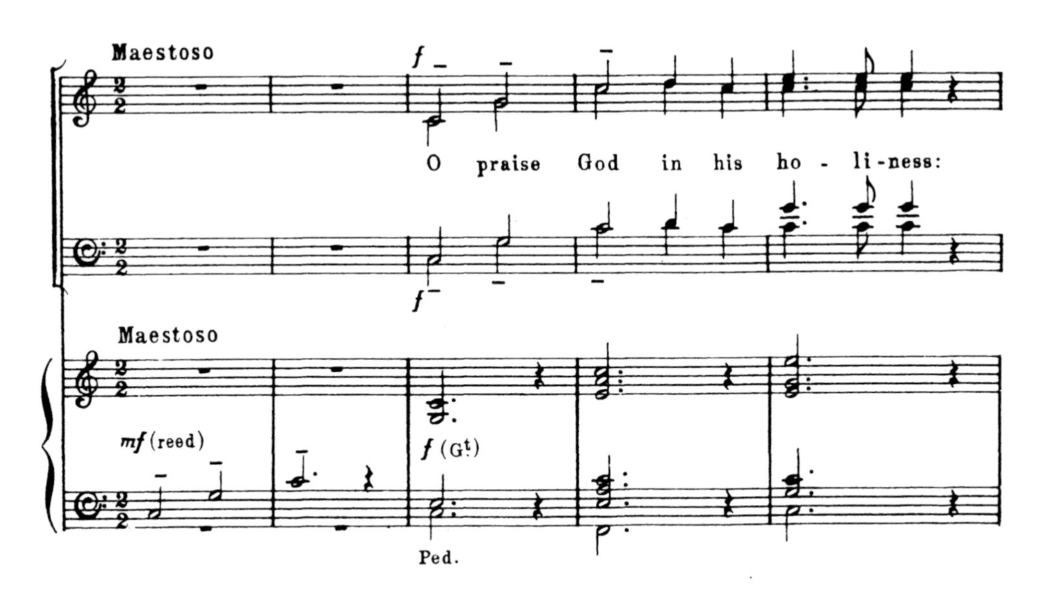
Maestoso
f
O praise God in his ho - li-ness:
f
Maestoso
mf (reed)
f (Gt)
Ped.

ff
praise him in the fir - ma-ment of his pow'r.
ff
ff

17

Maestoso
p
f
O - pen to me the gates of right-eous-ness,
p
f

them and I will praise the Lord.
mf
f
I will go in - to them and I will praise the Lord.
and I will praise the Lord.
mf
and I will praise the Lord.
f

18

Moderato
Our soul wait - eth for the Lord:
p
Our soul wait - eth for the Lord:
p

he is our help and our shield.
mf
mf
he is our help and our shield.

19

Andante
and grant us thy sal -
p
mf
Show us thy mer - cy, O Lord, and
mf
p
mf and grant us thy sal -

va - - - tion.
p
grant us thy sal - va - tion.
va - tion, sal - va - tion.
p

20

Moderato

21

Andante teneramente

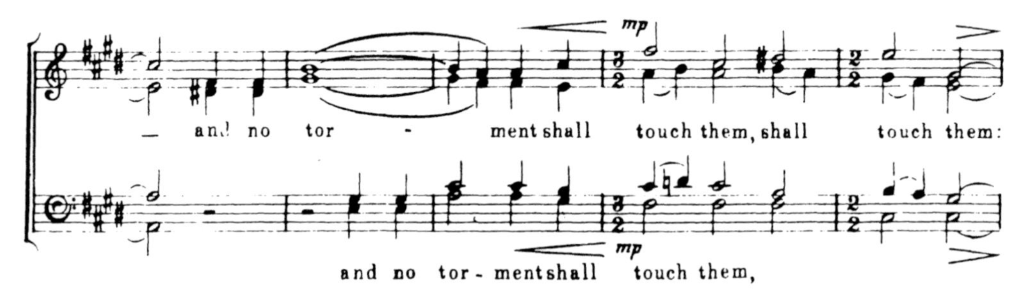

22

* Passages in brackets may be played on a solo reed

23

24

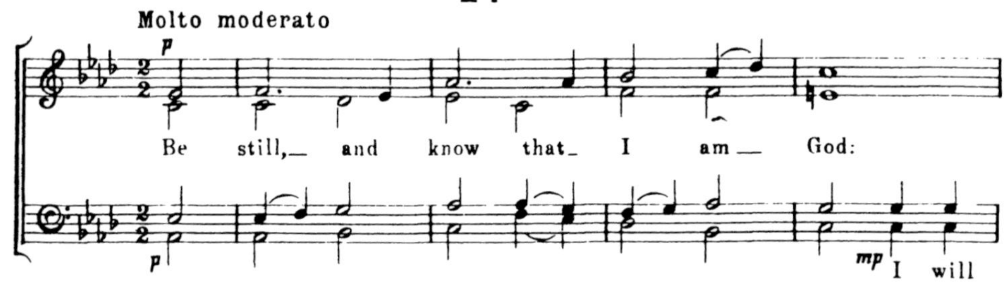

Printed in Great Britain

Novello
Publishing Limited
part of the Music Sales Group
14/15 Berners Street
London WIT 3LJ
DISTRIBUTED BY HAL LEONARD
8 84088 42272 1
14036898
Order No. NOV030105
5 020679 212592

ISBN-13: 978-0-85360-429-7
Distributed By
HAL LEONARD
14036898
9 780853 604297